GET THE MESSAGE?

GET THE MESSAGE?

BY DAN HARMAN

The Warner Press
Anderson, Indiana

COVER DESIGN BY J. DAVID LIVERETT

PRINTED IN THE UNITED STATES OF AMERICA

To Zena Church,
a special kind of Christian,
who demonstrates she "got the message"
by the way she lovingly shares it.

Acknowledgments

The author warmly thanks the following publications for permission to pass along portions of articles originally published under his by-line in their periodicals:

Child Evangelism Magazine
Christian Leadership
The Evangelical Beacon
The Gospel Herald (Cleveland, Ohio)
The Gospel Herald (Scottdale, Pa.)
The Herald of Holiness
The Nazarene Standard
Straight
Success
Vital Christianity
The War Cry

In addition I must thank all the pastors, church leaders, friends, and neighbors who so generously admitted to "goofs" of their own and passed along the errors of their friends. Most remain anonymous for obvious reasons. Many names have been changed to protect those involved.

CONTENTS

Chapter I

I DON'T WORK, I'M A PREACHER

Jane was writing home after a month of marriage. She'd just come from church and was complaining to her mother.

"Mom, I love Tony, but what's wrong with him? All through the sirvice [Jane was poor at spelling] Tony kept falling asleep. When the preacher was speaking, I don't think Tony got the massage at all."

But Jane was wrong. *I've* heard her preacher, and I think Tony got a very fine "massage." His ears were massaged. His nerves were massaged. His soul was massaged. There wasn't much "message" at all in the sermons. Mostly massage.

Which is what it's all about—this book, I mean. Those simple little mistakes, goofs, blurps, slip-of-the-tongue happenings that somehow have a way of saying what we don't want said, yet what needs to be said.

Of course, this isn't a new idea, revealing truth through error (the "Freudian slip" is an accepted part of psychology), but let's take a look at some of the mistakes and try to get messages from them.

Ever heard someone say, "He's got it soft. He's a preacher"? Maybe *you've* said it yourself. Most people sooner or later express some envy of the minister's work schedule. He's paid "too much for just two sermons a week."

I didn't help things much when I was a young man in the ministry. One day a visiting worker from the community asked me where I worked. "Oh, I don't work. I'm a preacher," I blurted out. Took me a long time to live that down.

But—in keeping with the spirit of this book—I believe that the ministers of our world share one general fear: that we're not giving God his week's work for the week's blessings he gives us. Too often we feel we don't work, we're preachers.

A MINISTER'S WORK

Let's look at a few bloopers and a few thoughts about the ministry. Let's see if they tell us anything about the pastor's work.

Assuredly, a pastor has to be a leader. By the nature of his work, he *is* a leader. For better or worse, worthy or not, a pastor leads. And a good pastor has something beyond this mere credential of his calling. He's more than a preacher. He's a leader who has a plus to his life, a special dimension that indeed makes him a modern "parson" to the community.

12

There's an unmistakable sparkle about a good pastor. Oh, it isn't a superficial glamor but rather a quality that wears well, inspires imitation, and tends to draw others to the church and Christ's way.

Ross Minkler is such a man. During many years of active ministry through his popular Green Pastures radio broadcast, he served the church-at-large from his base in Louisville, Kentucky. But, as come to all such fine leaders, there were times of being put in his place by odd events.

Like the time the post office delivered to him a letter that was simply addressed, The Shady Green Pastor, Louisville, Kentucky.

Being a pastor demands that we be "in season" all the time. Just a short lapse of memory can cause havoc. One pastor—in the heyday of opposition to playing cards—bowed over a sick bed and solemnly prayed for a Mr. McMaster, but called him "Mister Canasta."

And laymen reveal their deep feelings about their pastors in similar lapses of thought. A Wayne, Pennsylvania church paper stated, "We regret to report that the pastor does not plan to be away over any Sundays this summer." How nice it is in summertime to know the pastor is away on vacation and then the laymen, too, can feel free to be gone! How sad when these plans are dashed by an overzealous pastor!

Another such lapse in speech affected Keith

Huttenlocker, a gifted pastor in Indiana. The chairman introducing him to the audience announced, "Reverend Huttenlocker has a good education, but it hasn't gone to his head."

Another pastor, well-known for both his busy schedule and his weight-gaining pattern, was introduced to an audience with this explanation, "He's so busy, but he keeps gaining weight. It must be that he's burning the candle at both ends and the wax is running to the middle."

What does a pastor do? He gets along well with people in order to lead them, teach them, and challenge them to dedicate their lives to the evangelistic task of the church. Sometimes this getting-to-know-you task gets out of hand. Like the pastor who was told by a timid, but beautiful, lady. "Why , I'm so shy that I sometimes want to hide in the dark behind some door."

Absentmindedly—or was it?—the pastor answered, "Yes, I know how you feel. Sometimes I'd like to be there with you."

A pastor also works together with other pastors and Christian workers to get the larger job done. In committees, boards, commissions, and action groups, something is supposed to get done about the work, something too big for any one group to do alone. But these aims sometimes go astray. Much more talk than action. And the office seekers come to the front.

In one such gathering in Idaho some years ago, power seekers gained control of an area group and bossed the pastors around in various ways. But the pastors revolted. A bill was passed through the ministerial group stating clearly that, "The Executive Committee is to be subservient to the ministers."

Alas, when the printed minutes were distributed to the ministers at the next meeting, the secretary had stated the bill as saying, "The executive committee is subversive to the ministry."

And all this rushing around that ministers often do can be self-defeating. No matter where a pastor is, he is needed somewhere else. His mind often is two jumps ahead of his body. When at home, he's thinking about visiting; when he's in one home, he's thinking about the next one.

The perfect illustration was the pastor who phoned the airline for information.

"How long does it take to get to Chicago?" he asked.

Turning aside to consult a schedule, the clerk answered, "Just a minute, please."

Without thinking further about the answer, the pastor said, "Thank you," and hung up. Fast trip!

Service is the task of the pastor and character is his badge of office. One pastor dashed both in one stroke as he tried to glory in the work of the church and the ministry by quoting Jesus' analysis of "casting out devils and raising people from the dead." Unfortunately he said, "Our work is to cast out the dead and raise the devil."

AND I'M MOSES

And many pastors are confronted by their own irrationalities; they preach and work and encourage a standard that often trips them. Reportedly, John Haggai, a nationally known evangelist, was driving on a freeway in his hometown, accompanied by his associate, a Mr. Solomon. But, alas, he was stopped for speeding.

The officer asked for his license and Haggai answered as he handed it over, "Officer, I'm Haggai, like in the Bible, and this is my associate, Mr. Solomon." He naturally supposed that the intelligent officer knew of his reputation and standing in the community, but the officer stood straight-faced while he scanned the license. He showed no awareness of ministerial exemption from the laws of the state.

Clearing his throat, the evangelist gave it another try. "I'm Haggai, like in the Bible, and this is Solomon."

The officer slowly raised his eyes and answered firmly, "Well, Mr. Haggai—like in the Bible—I'm Moses and you've just broken the law." The chastened evangelist accepted the speeding ticket.

EXCHANGE PLACES?

But who'd want to exchange places with the pastor? Know anyone? Oh, there are lots of people who want to tell him what to do, who want to second-guess all he decides; people who think they know more about pastoring than a man who's doing it. But it's tough to get any of these to take over the reins.

The pastor and the church are in the midst of the roughest task ever imagined: the job of changing the characters of men and women.

The touching things that happen often make the pastor's task worthwhile; "But you don't look like a preacher," a young pastor was told by a hospitalized man who was near death. After they prayed, tears came to the man's eyes as he added, "But, thank God, you know Christ. I'll be all right now, thank you."

Or the pastor whose nightly prayer-times with his seven-year-old son became very precious. It was almost as though the boy was growing up in these quiet times by the bed. Then one night the pastor prayed quietly with his head right next to the boy's head. The boy's prayer followed, and as he prayed, he patted his father's shoulder. The father was moved deeply until he heard his son conclude his prayer with, "And, dear God, please help daddy not to have bad breath."

17

Chapter 2

THEY EXAMINED MY HEAD

Everyone knew what she meant, but the woman's words brought smiles to the faces of her friends. They *knew* her. And her poorly phrased report confirmed what they'd always thought. She'd been to the doctor for some of those vague "thobbings in my head."

The doctor examined her and she reported, "He looked at my head but he couldn't find anything." They'd always suspicioned that there was more vacuum than gray-matter in her head.

We all get caught by our own slipups, don't we? For a few minutes, let's look at the communication problem from the viewpoint, "Everyone seems stupid today, except me." All of us have felt this way, sometime or other, haven't we? We all get a little impatient with the slow driver, the uncertain sales clerk, the inattentive student, the boring professor.

How can we escape the communications trouble? How can we—the Christians of this earth—clearly tell what we mean in our attempted Christian communications? Through some "slips" let's see if we can find some help in Christian communications.

BE PATIENT

Probably one of the most needed reminders in the communications work of Christians is the need for a posted motto on every Christian's mirror, "Be Patient." (Or, as the man prayed, "Dear Lord, give me patience and give it to me right now!")

Patience is needed because we ourselves don't always say what we mean or mean what we say. Consider the church worship folder with this listing: "Congregational Hymn, 'Rise Up, O Men of God' (congregation please remain seated)." We all "goof," so we need patience with the other fellow who also goofs.

And what about the pastor who prays, "Father, give us a worshipful and meaningful service this morning, Amen." And then he proceeds to fill ten minutes with trivial and unimportant announcements. My wife quickly checks me with, "Cut out the jibber-jabber and let's worship." I'm thankful.

And we all say things we wish we hadn't said. If we do it, let's not be surprised when the other man does, too. Tolerate him. Work toward clear speaking and clear thinking yourself, and put up with other Christians who also have difficulty communicating clearly.

Practice makes perfect. Communicate as a witness

for Christ and not for yourself. Improve; be persistent with yourself.

DON'T BE AN EXPERT

Donna was a sweet girl. She was quiet, yet self-assured. Then doctors discovered a heart ailment that might cripple her. Everyone seemed frightened except Donna. Following serious surgery, she sat with the doctor, receiving her instructions on her future activities and health guards. She still refused to be as solemn as the doctor was.

"Now, Donna," he asked, "are there any questions you'd like to ask about your future?"

With a sober face, she replied, "Yes, doctor, now that I've had my surgery, will I be able to play the piano?"

"Why, of course, dear. There's no reason why you shouldn't."

Again her blank face masked her impish spirit. "Thank you, doctor. I never could play it before and it's comforting to know the surgery will enable me to play."

The doctor had taken himself too seriously. He'd left himself wide open for the patient who had her feet on the ground.

Be a worker-together with God. Be a channel through whom he works. Be a disciple, always following the Master. Be the best kind of Christian you can be, but *please* don't be an expert. You'll void all the good that might be done.

Let Christ be the expert. In communicating, rely on the Bible, on great writings of the ages, and on your own personal experiences to communicate Christ. Make a simple rule: "I will either tell people that which has personally happened to me, or I will direct them to an expert." Live this. Never consider yourself an expert. Notice how your communications improve for Christ.

CONSIDER THE PERSON

Look outward instead of inward when you tell others about Christ. Christian communications improve in direct ratio to our involvement with the well-being of the other fellow.

Notice, for instance, how much of the Christian faith is adult-centered. Many practices, beliefs, teachings, observances, and theological positions are too complicated to be put into children's terms. The Bible itself is basically an adult book. We have to have a "children's Bible" to make it meaningful to the little ones.

Consider this when you speak about Christ to others. Take note of the intelligence, age, cultural background, and experience of the people with whom you share Christ. It may be that you'll be most effective in proportion to what you don't say. It may also be true that you'll need many sessions and much question-and-answer time to help some folk.

Look at children again. Notice how often they repeat what they *think* they hear instead of what's said. Two examples jump out in relation to the Christmas story.

Telling the Bethlehem story, one little boy explained in some detail how the shepherds were on the hillside that historic night, very busily "washing their socks by night."

The other was a five-year-old who was asked to draw a picture of the first stable-home of Jesus' family. He drew Mary and Joseph very well, but added an exceptionally fat baby in the manger. Sharing his drawing, he pointed out the mother and father. "And who's that in the manger?" the teacher asked.

Staring at her uninformed face, the boy answered, "Why that's round John Virgin, of course."

Accept people for what they are, and witness to them from there. Communicate the spirit of Christ, rather than a set of facts. Many psuedo-Christian cults are brimful of highly complicated theology. They knock on our doors and try to sell us a new doctrine. Notice how few are really interested in our souls. They want to persuade us to believe their doctrines. Let's not communicate on that level. Let's care about individuals.

Let's care no matter how terrible their excuses. None could be quite as bad as the man who said he didn't attend church because he hated cheese. When asked what this had to do with church, he answered, "Oh, they're always singing about 'Bringing in the Cheese,' and it makes me sick."

Love them where they are and try to introduce them —with love and logic and common sense—to Christ. Communications that do not transmit love are faulty communications.

SETTLE FOR GETTING THROUGH

Too many of us want to be amateur lawyers. Settle, instead, for getting a hearing with our communications for Christ. Be ready to let God pick up where your voice leaves off. Give God something to work on when you're out of sight.

Say what you have to say and leave the rest to God. But beware of your hidden meanings, not like the TV preacher who spent ten minutes on camera reading letters from listeners, each time being sure the audience could see the cash attached to each letter. Then, in a most pleading voice, he turned toward the TV camera and addressed the viewers: " My dear funds. . . ."

Say it and give God a chance to work. God and others may very well do more with your words than you do. Or, to put it like one lady who came home to her husband after church and asked for $5. "Our pastor has resigned, dear, and the congregation wants to give him a little momentum."

24

At the conclusion of a worship service, a pastor asked the congregation to rise and called upon one of the laymen to pray the benedictory prayer. As the man arose, the opera seat arms of the chair in which he'd been seated hooked in the side pockets of his brand new coat and ripped them both.

As the pastor and congregation waited for the prayer, the man spoke out. "You better get someone else to pray. I just spent my last dime on this coat and I'm in no mood to pray."

You don't know what events have been experienced by the person you have just met. This can have many implications, but look at two. First, it may mean that nothing you say can help him right now. Things may have hit him in such a way that his heart is not receptive to Christian witness. Ask God for another opportunity. Don't force the issue.

But it may also mean something else. It may mean that the smallest, simplest, most poorly said communication imaginable will reach deep into the life of someone who hears you with open ears and an eager heart. No matter how badly you feel you're communicating, someone with a willing spirit can be blessed. Don't knock your own effectiveness, for often the other fellow is much more eager to hear what you have to say than you are to say it.

In the fullest sense of the term, we Christians "put up with" non-Christians so we can reach them for

Christ. We are not tucked away in some safe place, reserved for "Christians Only." We are out in the world, communicating for Christ. That's our place.

And often that place is right in our homes. People need to live for Christ right where they are. Most pointedly said, this comes out in the scene in a hotel lobby. A middle-aged man huffs and puffs into the giant room and leans on the desk clerk's counter. "Got any rooms where I can put up with my wife?" he asks.

That's about it sometimes. Communicating the gospel is often simply seeking someplace where we can "put up with" those around us in order that we may reach them for our Master. It's not easy, but it can be done.

Chapter 3

YOU HAVE TO BE BALD

Carroll Dale, pro football player, is bald. Some may call it "thinning hair" or a "high forehead," but the truth is he's bald. A little boy asked him why he'd lost his hair.

"When I first joined the Packers," Carroll answered, "I wanted to do anything to gain acceptance, so I went to Ray Nitschke and asked his advice." Ray is a burly football star who for years has frightened the opposition with his power and courage. But Ray is nearly skinned on top.

"Ray told me I should be bold when I played, but I thought he said bald. So I shaved off my hair and I've been bald ever since." Carroll said it with a grin and the boy understood the joke.

But we in the church have often mouthed phrases about power, then demonstrated about as much strength as there is hair on a bald head.

Power for the Christian comes through the Holy Spirit, his infilling, his guidance, and his daily presence. But the need for this power is something the Christian world must be sold on before the Spirit will act. If we don't want him, he won't empower us. With the help of a few goofs that are normal for us humans, let's take a look at our need of power and see if we "get the message."

Weak and Puny

Describing the inadequacies of mortals is a regular pastime of satirists. One pastor, in a message on the needs of mankind, blurted out that we are a race of "puke and weeny men." Or as one typographical error said it, "he has a worm personality, and a low, pleasant voice."

People, when left to their own devices, turn out to be less than what we want them to be. It takes the power of God in man to make man what he can become on this earth.

And if we add the spiritual dimension of attaining love and brotherhood among the peoples of earth, then only the Prince of Peace can bring this about. Without God we truly are "puke and weeny."

Doctors can repair the body, counselors can help us adjust to life around us, psychiatrists can try to root out troubles that handicap us, but each is limited.

Or as one tongue-in-cheek advertisement phrased the promise of a famous psychiatrist, "Positive cure in two years or your mania back."

Each man, as he tries to help his fellowman, is limited. Only God and his power in a life can lift it above its fate and make it what he intended it to be.

28

We as individuals must (1) face ourselves, (2) seek God's view of our spiritual condition, (3) let him push out of our lives anything that's unworthy of a Christian, (4) invite the Holy Spirit of God to come in, and (5) believe in faith that he gives his Spirit to us. Read your Bible: Luke 11:13 mentions God's eagerness to share his Spirit.

THE CHURCH OF GO

The First Church of God in New Boston, Ohio, has a lovely building. But a few years ago they worshipped in a crowded brick building that was built right to the edge of the sidewalk. In fact the front wall was so close to the curb that the church sign in front of the building had to be hung with part of the sign hidden from view of passersby.

The sign read simply, "First Church of God." But as people drove by, all they could see was, "First Church of Go. . . ."

Folks used to kid members about it till one alert pastor came back with, "Would you rather we were the 'Church of Stop'?"

And that's the kind of power we need in the church: Go-power. That's the kind we often feel is missing. We see a fine building, pleasant faces, children all around; yet we sense that the church isn't going anywhere or doing anything.

Too often we feel: "My church is so weak that a good stiff wind would blow it away." So often we are fearful that a first-class persecution would take every Christian in sight out of the church.

Personal power is the first step to take in remedying the situation. But let me suggest a few more.

(1) Pray together with any other Christian you can find that the church will gain a new desire for better communications, more love, and a soul burden. Prayer is the key. Prayer for the basic ingredients that will make the power of the Holy Spirit in the assembled fellowship necessary is the second step in this prayer. When people sense a need for God's personal intervention, they'll get ready for him.

Good communication is vital. One elderly visitor to New Orleans had dreamed all his life of visiting the famous city. Walking down an ancient street, he looked up to see Spanish moss hanging from the old trees. His eyes brightened. "Look, Maud. There's some of that 'Marty-grass' we've heard about for so long."

Getting to know each other is vital to having the Holy Spirit visit a congregation with his power.

Clearing the air follows getting to know each other. Each congregation has a segment of Christians who need sweetening up. They need what the little boy prayed for: "Dear God, please make all the bad people good and all the good people nice."

Working toward the ideal of 1 Corinthians 13 is next. Let everyone who seeks God's power for the congregation join together in prayer that each may learn to truly love the others, as Christ loved us, and died for us.

(2) When the circle of concerned people is large enough, launch an informal campaign toward uniting the congregation in seeking God's will for that congregation. Pray, discuss, brainstorm, share, ask, and seek. Evaluate past work. See what others are doing. Give God every chance to help the group see what he wants of you.

(3) Narrow down the concerns to one thing the people can do together in a united effort: a missions project, a building program, a visitation program, a new evangelistic thrust, a community service project, a search for Sunday school leaders: in most churches the list of available needs far exceeds the personnel to carry them out. Select one need and get behind it.

Be enthusiastic. Trust God that what you undertake will be successful. Be optimistic. Get to the place where you have to ask God's Spirit to empower the situation, because you expect so much from it.

Let your excitement show. One pastor, weary of facing a congregation of people who successfully hid their feelings, blurted out, "Why, if there were one healthy 'amen' in this building, some of you would pass out. We'd have to get the epsom salts for you." That he meant "smelling salts" was beside the point. He felt the church was dead anyhow.

Go out on a limb, trusting God's power to make things move. Trusting the Holy Spirit to help you do that which you've asked him to direct makes your church a "church of go."

The phone rang in the church office. A lady asked, "Do you have any firewood for sale?" The pastor let her know she had the wrong number, but as he replaced the phone, he thought out loud, "Perhaps we ought to have lots of fuel for distribution to weak people of our community—spiritual fuel."

POWER OUTSIDE THE CHURCH

There is much to be said for God's demonstrations of power within the church itself. But—as the pastor above felt— there ought to be something happen to the community if the Holy Spirit touches a congregation.

Up in Berryville, Virginia, in beautiful Shenandoah country, is a church building. It stands at one end of the block; at the far end is the local electric power plant. In a narrow alley between them the cars park on Sunday. It's but a few feet from the front door of the church to the high fence that protects people from the high voltage wires and coils and transmitters that keep the lights on in Berryville. It's a power plant right next to a church building.

The first time I saw it, I thought, That church must be spiritually dead—all the power's next door.

Then I remembered Jesus' command: "Ye shall receive power. . . . Ye shall be my witnesses," The demonstration of power was not what happened of a spectacular nature within the confines of the building, but what happened to the country outside the building when the power was turned loose there.

If you think the local congregation where you worship is short on power, check into the outreach. Specifically, do they give sacrificially to missions? (Or are they taken up with their own problems?)

Do they actively reach out to the surrounding community with a warm, urgent, concerned welcome? (Or do they say by their attitude, "We're here. If they want to come to church, let them come"?)

Sometimes the surrounding community has a very peculiar view of the local congregation. We think highly of ourselves, but what do our actions tell the people of the neighborhood?

A newsnote in a paper recently observed, "The people of Columbia, Tennessee—the largest outdoor mule market in the world—held a jackass parade yesterday, headed by the governor." Now, that's not what they meant. But it's what the paper said!

Power is this: personal, from the Holy Spirit to you by his infilling; it is in the church by the concerted efforts of members to welcome him and allow him to use them; it is outside the church as the Spirit impells us to take the gospel to the whole world.

Chapter 4

GET THE RIGHT GOD

The roadside cross-shaped sign was familiar. It was there to warn motorists to beware of their spiritual condition. It was supposed to say, "Get Right With God," but the arm of the cross that was supposed to contain the "with" was broken off. It made the sign say, "Get Right God." I laughed at it, but then I agreed. There are millions of people serving the wrong god; they, indeed, need to get the right one.

Values are a rather hard-to-define set of things, aren't they? The standards by which we live change and are refined so often that it's hard to pin them down. The modern temptation is to say, "Everything's relative. There is no absolute right or wrong."

Let's look at values, for the Christian of our day is so apt to complain, "Where *is* God anyhow? Does he still care about me?"

SIN BY CANDLELIGHT

A youth manual for leaders gives this instruction in connection with a quiet worship service: "Let the youth sin softly by candlelight." Standing up for the right, having principles in broad daylight is tough. The temptation is to "sin softly" in the dark. Keep quiet about our beliefs and do as we please. Just don't hurt anyone, that's enough.

Holding strong moral and ethical positions is tough. That's the first lesson to learn about values.

So many things cry out for change and improvement. It's so hard to care when we look around and see so many who don't seem to get excited or concerned about anything. One man up Illinois way erected his own sign on a county road, after he complained for years about its poor condition. "Drive carefully. This road should be under construction."

But the Christian must face the tough task of holding high values and getting the right things at the head of the list. It's a rough task. Sometimes just doing what comes naturally is so tempting.

Roscoe was a fine man. He had grown old, and many members of his family had passed on ahead of him. He called his pastor one day and invited him out to the little farm for lunch. Roscoe lived alone, and he felt he was a burden on his children, especially after arthritis kept him from doing his work.

"Pastor," he said while they were eating, "tell me something. Is it wrong for a Christian to commit suicide?"

The pastor nearly dropped his cracker. The very idea was so unlike Roscoe. Then the pastor began to see. To keep from being a burden on his children, Roscoe thought the kindest thing was just not to be there anymore.

Kindly, quietly, the pastor tried to explain that God gives life and so long as life remains, God has something for the Christian to do. But through it all, the pastor sensed that Roscoe's motives were pure and unselfish. Doing right, holding the highest values can be a touchy, difficult job sometimes.

I saw a former college classmate of mine the other day. Her face brought back the memory of a lilting laugh, a bright smile, eyes whose sparkle was loved by many on the campus. Then I looked at the woman before me. Gone were the sparkling eyes. Now she was gray, and haggard lines carved furrows across her face. She looked tired.

After the usual review of our lives in the years between, she pulled out a stack of photos. "These are my children," she said with a kindness that was poetic. I looked at the faces. "God has been good to me. They're wonderful children." In the boy's face I saw her dazzling smile. In the girl's look I saw the sparkling eyes. Their happy grins reminded me of my classmate just a few years back.

Then it dawned on me. What I had taken for a wasted, ruined life was simply a misunderstanding on my part. She hadn't worn those lines in her face by misuse of her life. She'd exchanged her youth and beauty for the rewarding task of rearing her children to know Christ. She'd passed along her vitality to those she loved the best. It was a difficult exchange, but a warm and wonderful one. In each child I saw the best of her. She'd made an angelic trade.

SPIRITUAL BRINKMANSHIP

"Every child of God is able to defeat the world," is the assertion of 1 John 5:4, TEV*. How often we let the world get right on top of us; it weighs us down. Our values are clouded and our dreams are muddied. Then, in a burst of faith, in a flash of trust in God, victory is snatched from the jaws of defeat. A quick lifting of the heart to God in a moment of real faith can alter a situation in a moment.

This "spiritual brinkmanship" is a constant danger to the Christian. Values can be preserved only when we are willing to skirt the very edge of disaster to redeem them. We must be prepared to act or die. "Give me liberty or give me death" was a motto the revolutionists used. Christians must echo the sentiments. We hold on to our values and we put shoes on them or we lose out, spiritually.

My wife detests cigarette smoke. She's tried my patience many times by going out of her way to make people who smoke feel uncomfortable. She has a low "R.P." That's the short way of saying she can smell

*From the Today's English Version of the New Testament. Copyright © American Bible Society, 1966.

smoke a mile away. Her "revolting point" is a low one. She revolts quickly and claims she has a right to breathe unpolluted air.

Maybe more of us ought to be spiritually offended more easily. Maybe we should stand up more forthrightly for the things we believe. Our souls may be strengthened if we look for opportunities to witness to our strong faith.

And churches must guard against lowering their values. As units of people joined together by the saving love of Christ, congregations must act or die.

An advertisement in a church magazine caught my eye not long ago. It was for a new type of upholstered church chair that absorbed sound. The key line was, "With this chair, the sound in the sanctuary will be the same as if it were filled with people." Just the kind of compromise we need: chairs that sound like people.

In every area of life we find confrontations with right and wrong. We must act when action is called for.

The new highway was coming right through a lovely residential section of town. It was hard to see the expensive lawns and shrubbery torn up. Many homeowners removed what they could.

One bulldozer operator must have felt a heartthrob, too, as his implement scraped away the dreams and efforts of beauty-loving people. Finally, able to stand his own destruction no longer, he wheeled his 'dozer, unearthed a perfectly formed lilac bush, lifted it high in the air, dirt and all, and headed through town. Townspeople stopped to stare at the sight of the lilac-bush-laden bulldozer charging right through the business district till he dumped it in the center of town on a grassplot. There, methodically, he dug a hole and carefully planted the bush. As he drove away, the bellow of his engine was drowned out by the spontaneous applause of the townspeople.

JUST GET ME OUT

The final thing about values that we must face is the promise of God that if we stay true, hold high the Christian way, if we are good soldiers, we will be rewarded.

God rewards those who stay true. No matter how we tend to feel that God has deserted modern peoples, he hasn't. He's in charge. He rewards those who stay faithful.

Read Isaiah 63:7. It says something we often overlook in daily life. It says that God rewards us according to *his* lovingkindness. Not according to our ability to receive. Not according to our ideas of what that lovingkindness ought to be. But the Almighty's boundless resources are there to be given as he decides. He is not just powerful enough to send sinners to everlasting hell. He's powerful enough to reward his faithful children according to omnipotent dimensions. His blessings are beyond our comprehension. Remember this when it seems hard to follow him.

And only God can properly reward you. A few years ago I regularly visited the Indiana State Prison in Michigan City. Each time the men seemed to enjoy the break from routine. But each time they tugged at my heartstrings by their request.

To a man, without exception, each time our visiting hour was over, they made the same request. I'd ask, "Well, is there anything I can do for you?"

Each time the answer came back. With sad eyes and set jaw, each man would say, "Yes, preacher. Just get me out of here."

And I'd have to answer, "Men, I'll do anything I can. But that's one thing I haven't the power to do."

The marvelous thing is that God *can* set us free from the sins and burdens of this life. He can reward us. He can lift our hearts. Our holding on to the Christian way gives God the opening he loves. He can shower us with blessings and renew our spirits as never possible with anyone else.

All we have to do is be faithful and ask.

A sign in a Montreal restaurant says, "Early bird gets the worm. Special shopper's luncheon before 11 A.M." Now that's not the kind of reward we want. But those who pitch in at an early age do reap more rewards than those who wait.

Those who forsake the values of the Bible reap their reward, too. One pastor boldly warned his people about going on picnics instead of coming to church

41

services. He expressed his feeling so pointedly that he almost red-faced himself out of the church.

He expressed it this way, and rescued himself: "If any of you go on a picnic instead of coming to church, I hope you get ants in your p-p-p-p-picnic."

Christian values are clear in the Bible. To apply them in our day is no easy task. But the heartfelt decision to live by the rules that God has laid down is essential. We cannot take the liberty to set down our own values. Loyalty to God's word must come first. If we err on the side of being behind the times, we may come closer to being acceptable in God's sight than if we err by taking Christian values into our own hands and contradicting God.

Chapter 5

PRAY OPEN THE OFFERING

"All they ever talk about at church is money." Heard someone say that recently? "Money, money, money. That's all our pastor ever thinks of."

The Saginaw, Michigan, *News* recently printed a brief report that strikes a note of understanding: "The pastor at Mt. Carmel Church told police someone attempted to pray open an offering table coin box." Everything concerning money in that church must have been tightly sealed! Perhaps in the thief's attempt to pry open the box, he did resort to prayer.

What place *does* money have in the church? Should every church try to be debt free? Is interest paid on loans a waste of money that should be going to God?

There's no way to answer every question about money and the church, but a look at some key factors might help. It doesn't help to fuss about money in the church: there ought to be a constructive approach to finances. It's like a problem that one New York church had when weddings produced a fine layer of confetti over the church lawn on summer Saturdays—a layer that was never gone by Sunday. The church finally placed on the lawn a sign designed to make the most of a losing battle. It read: "If you must throw something at the bride, try throwing grass seed."

KNOW YOUR NEIGHBORS

The first factor is a simple one, but one that so many church people never learn: get to know the people who worship with you. Get to know them in love. Know the ones who talk too much. Get to know the silent ones who support the finances of the church quietly but persistently. Know the talk-big-give-little ones.

They're all different, you know. Different, just as you're different from them. Know them and make allowances for them.

Some speak too quickly about money. Like the teen-age bride who woke up one morning after six months of marriage complaining, "Sometimes I think I married too young. I went right from homework to housework."

Some people are all for an idea—one that involves money—until it comes time to pay the bill. Then they back off. They get involved in something else. Some are reactors. They don't have a new idea and will never have one. They stay quiet until someone suggests something, then they react.

Or worse, they vote to spend money in the church, and then forever complain that "I never did believe in it," after the decision is reached and the pleas for funds come along.

Get to know people—in love! Don't criticize them or hold hard feelings against them. Get to know them, and hear them with a knowing ear. When the "talk-big-give-little" people speak out, filter their views. When the quiet ones who give steadily speak, listen carefully. Let the decisions about money be made democratically but wisely.

There will be those who speak now and think later. One man—who knew his fellow churchmen quite well—got tired of hearing one of these often-speaking, non-thinking men say he was "going to bat" for a special money-oriented project. After the third time of hearing the man say he was "going to bat for it," the wise churchman jumped to his feet and said, "That's three strikes, you're out." And the meeting continued.

KEEP UP HOME BASE

We hear a lot these days about "putting our money to work in missions" instead of in building new and larger church buildings. And this is a needed area of study. Too many churches are self-centered. If the local bills are paid and the building is a fine showplace for visitors, then we will give from the overflow to missions. This idea needs drastic changing.

But to follow some people's theories on money would be disaster of another sort. While we're raising money for overseas missions, we must keep the home base strong. The local church must pay for itself and do all it can to keep all the members sharing in the costs of the local operation. There are some checks and balances that can be brought to bear.

First, are complete records kept and published? Do the people know where their money is going? I believe in tithing and giving above the tithe, but one of the best ways to get people to want to give to the church is to show them where the money goes.

Next, are the people who have charge of spending the money known and trusted? To give a man who can't manage his personal finances a strong voice in managing God's money is folly. He neither merits nor will get the support of the people, no matter how the pastor speaks on giving to God.

Finally, does the church as a whole have the final say-so on all monies spent? This doesn't have to be on a bill-by-bill basis. The congregation can delegate the responsibility to a board or committee. But can the church speak and counteract any decision? This gives people a feeling of control. And it can give the finance leaders a foothold to ask the church's prayerful consideration of the plans.

Strengthen the home base and then launch out: that's one of the basic keys to financial success in the church. Maurice Berquist, of Daytona Beach, once asked his congregation, "Are you a Christian or a sanctified worrier?" When it comes to money, this also is a vital question. To do God's will in faith is to commit the results to him. Never worry about money in the local church if both the plans and the people and the money-raising are in his hands.

KEEP YOUR PRIORITIES

The third factor that needs attention is the matter of priorities in church finance. Each congregation has to set its own. No dictates from outside or considerations of what another church is doing will help. Do it yourself, under God's direction.

Decide what bills are to be paid first, second, third, in order of priority. Consider who will contribute and who will withhold. Don't set the budget so high it can't be reached. Remember that the people in the pews will furnish the money.

You'll have people like the one the pastor spoke about in his congregation. When asked about the parishoner's giving, the pastor said, "Oh, he'll give till it hurts, but he is very sensitive to pain."

And people will misunderstand the budget. Make it as plain as you can. Get the people behind the budget because it's their budget and they understand it. Then spend according to the priorities you have agreed upon.

47

One national church leader who worked on an evangelism committee received a letter addressed to the *Committee on Inter-Church Vandalism*. It may be that the writer had something on his mind about the ethics of the committee, or he may have been ignorant. But too many of our money-spending groups in the church are not understood well enough to gain support.

Inform and then stick to the plan of spending. This constant and methodical approach to church finances builds a trust in the giver that helps him give, even when it hurts. It develops a feeling of positive assurance that the money is being spent to the best advantage.

Missions should be high up on the list of priorities. But the idea of informing and repeating the information is vital. Most church groups have a cooperative body that organizes the total giving of the church body: some for colleges, some for evangelism, some for poverty area churches, some for overseas outreach.

One Protestant group calls its cooperative organization World Service, since it encompasses many varied educational, benevolent, and mission efforts. One congregation that had been giving for years obviously had given in ignorance of the real use of the money. The national office received a notice which read "We have give to that World Service church long enough. It should be self-supporting by now. We ain't going to give anymore."

48

People who come to believe in the financial pattern of a church get behind the work. Often the uninformed, the newcomer, is as full of enthusiasm for the work as is the old-timer who has come through a lot in the years past.

DON'T BE SELF-CONSCIOUS

There's no use getting too self-conscious about money. Everyone has to handle it and use it. It is a natural part of the work of the church.

One Sunday a pastor was faced with a hushed congregation, waiting for the offertory prayer. The floor of the sanctuary was slanted, and just as the ushers paused before the altar for prayer, a small boy in the rear dropped his handful of coins and they came clattering down the incline toward the front, rolling and jangling. Many gasped, wondering what the pastor would say.

"Thank you, son. Following our prayer, we'll take a second offering if you please."

And remember, there'll always be those who will oppose everything the church does, in finances as well as every other area. They want to be a part of the church without functioning. This spirit was summed up in the complaint of one man: "I can't understand that church. They have never elected me to one office in all these years. I can't understand it unless it's because I seldom attend and never give a penny."

Chapter 6

THINE IS THE HOUR

His voice was a little shaky, but the teacher was sure Buddy could say the Lord's Prayer. Then she heard him say, "Thine is the kingdom, the hour and the glory." After the prayer, she wanted to correct him, but something in his words challenged her. She was supposed to make the "hour" God's hour; that was her job. Maybe Buddy's prayer should be her prayer: "God, make this Sunday school class *thy* hour."

Children shake us up and dare us to live what we teach, don't they? It's almost as though they expect the Christian life to be full of adventure. But, well, maybe that's what's wrong with many so-called Christians' lives: they've let the adventure slip away.

In Junior Camp the boys and girls were asked to list at random the greatest Bible heroes. A list of some forty resulted. Know who the top three were? (1) Jesus, (2) God, and (3) Babe Ruth. I think the youngsters were trying to tell the counselors something, don't you? One life to live. Let it be filled with God's greatest adventures.

Too often we adults want to stifle adventuring spirits as soon as we spot them. One teen-ager was overheard telling her friend, "Yesterday I developed a whole new personality, but daddy made me wash it off."

KEEP THE LIGHT OFF

A few years back I came across the custodian of the church sweeping a long hall in total darkness. "Want me to switch the light on for you?" I asked.

"My goodness, no," he answered seriously. "Then I could see the dirt."

Some Christians are like that. They know there's adventurous living out there, but they put the blinders on. They don't want the kind of adventures Christ has for us. We of our own accord make the Christian life dull and wearisome. As Lincoln said, "People in general tend to be as happy as they make up their minds to be." Life with Christ isn't boring or tedious unless we make it so.

Almost anyone with a wee bit of faith can find excitement in following the Nazarene. Or—to stretch it a bit—we can almost be like the news headline: "Cemetery Gets Praise from Former Resident."

And our dull, lifeless, uninteresting lives are seen by others. They get to know what the church is like by observing us. A report of a concert says a lot about this kind of example: "A tenor soloist sang, 'I Shall

Not Pass This Way Again,' much to the delight of the audience."

Christians *are* witnesses. We can witness to the vital, contagious, fully-alive Spirit of Christ within us, or we can demonstrate that Christ has given us nothing worth getting excited about, nothing worth recommending to others.

THIS WAY TO HEAVEN

Being at-one with Christ is an adventure. But one caution: remember that living the Christian life and joining with Jesus to win the world is the toughest single job ever imagined by man or God. The church is trying to do the hardest thing ever tried: we're trying to change the basic nature of man himself. Of course, we do not do it alone, but the job is so enormous that we ought not expect to come out unscarred and completely satisfied. It will be a long, hard climb and the price will be great. Many will fall by the wayside and many will go unconverted. But the adventure of being in on the gigantic challenge is beyond words.

An advertisement in a Chicago radio commercial caught my ear some time back. It was for an insurance firm and the pitch was that having their insurance "takes the IF out of LIFE." It's a catchy idea for insurance, but it runs afoul of the aims of Christ when we apply it to living.

Jesus came to make all of life "iffy" if we follow him. No person is safe. No cause is easy. No challenge light. "If" may be the one greatest handicap of the Christian life.

We can get to heaven, if! We can win others, if! We can pray the prayer of healing for the sick, if! The whole scheme of living by faith is a huge "IF."

Charley is a large, powerful man. As a plumber, he's tops. No job is too tough, no work too dirty, no family too poor for Charley. He's built a business on a reputation of honesty, thoughtfulness, and quality workmanship.

Some time back Charley, a thoroughly Christian gentleman, became involved with the Internal Revenue Service. On advice from his accountant he had filed what turned out to be erroneous income forms. When he tried to correct them, the federal service decided to "make an example" of him. Without going into detail, the whole thing ended up with Charley being sentenced to a year in prison. The stunning blow to his life and the lives of his family, friends, and church was shattering. "No! Anyone but Charley," was heard all around town. "Let me go in his place," dozens offered. The church began to pray. Everyone knew that something had to be done to rescue him from this situation.

But time passed, and the very night before he was to surrender himself to the marshall, Charley was in church. As he bowed at the altar, tears of sympathy flowed from the eyes of many in the crowded sanctuary. As he stood to say a word, people were all praying, "Please, God, keep Charley out of jail."

But Charley knew the Christian life was tough. His words were simple but profound. "I've finally prayed through," he said in his quiet, even voice. "I've got it figured out. For me, the way to heaven runs through that prison. Now, I want to go to heaven, so I'd be a fool to go any way except the way that leads there." A tough decision, but a deep surrender.

Charley spent two weeks behind bars and then was freed by an unprecedented court order. No one could explain it. "I can," he said. "It was simply God's will that I be released." He insisted, "No one said following Christ would be easy."

There's something tough you can do right where you are. An unknown poet has penned the challenge this way:

> He placed me in a little cage, away from gardens fair;
> But I must sing the sweetest songs because he placed me there.
> Not beat my wings against the cage, if it's my Maker's will,
> But raise my voice to heaven's gate and sing the louder still.

HE WON'T STAY THROWED

There's a rich adventure in Christ just around the corner for you. It's part of you, if you're his. Sometimes the going's tough and the odds are against you, but you know from past experience that sticking to it is everything.

They tell a story down in Tennessee about Andy Jackson as a boy: thin, freckle-faced, wiry, and ready to take on anyone.

A gang of boys jumped him and after they'd pretty well knocked him around, they walked off. In a flash Andy was back on his feet, chasing after them. One boy said to another, "You go back and throw him down again." The selected one went back. After a flurry of dust, punches, and grunts, Andy threw the boy back into the gang.

"What's the matter?" the leader demanded of his buddy.

"Well," the answer came back, "I throw him, but he won't stay throwed."

The stick-with-it, never-say-die spirit of adventure lifts the heart. The word "soaring" often describes the heart of the Christian involved in the adventure of following Christ.

Stuart Hamblen penned a beautiful description:

> The soul of man is like a soaring falcon,
> When it's released, it's destined for the sky.

Ever think of the beauty of a forest? It's shady, comfortable, lovely to see. Birds find protection, food, and a place to raise their young. But what of the eagle? No safe and secure forest for him. If you put him there he'd wing his way up and out and soon soar high above the trees. There's just something in him that shuns the safety and comfort of the woods, and calls him to soar on high. When the Holy Spirit came at Pentecost, he didn't bid the disciples to rent a room and enjoy the Gift. He bade them venture out to preach and dare.

Each of us needs a venture for Christ. We hope it isn't in the manner of a church bulletin's report: "Tonight after the evening service the adults will meet for a get-acquainted period. Each one is asked to bring a sandwich. The drink will be provided. This could be a high hour together."

Or the venture as described by the Swiss guide in the Alps: "Be careful, as you view this scene," he said, pointing to a dangerous overlook. "The footing is nasty. Be sure you don't fall, but if you do, remember to look to the right as you fall, for the view is extraordinary!"

The great preacher, Spurgeon, once told of a giant oak tree in a forest. It did a magnificent job of protecting a tiny sapling that took root at its base. The sapling was so thankful that the giant tree kept the winds and hail from harming it. In each storm the sapling again and again expressed its gratitude to the sturdy oak. Then an especially harsh storm struck and the giant oak was felled by the fury of the gale.

"O, what shall I do?" the sapling said. But, with the shade of the oak gone, the sun beamed down upon the sapling. The rains fed its roots and the tiny tree began to grow. The extra room left by the felling of the oak turned out to be a blessing. Soon it was tall and strong, and when the storms came, the sapling was big enough to withstand the storm on its own.

Is there anything except the launching out that keeps you and me from deeper paths with Christ? Perhaps, if we dared more to do his will, we, too, would be stronger and better able to cope with life.

Chapter 7

THE DUMB PREACHER'S WIFE

"You know, he'd be a good preacher if it weren't for his wife."

Ever heard that? Ever felt that way? Ever looked at a pastor—or your pastor—and thought it? Lots of people have. Lots of people feel that way and it hurts (1) the church, (2) the pastor and his wife, and (3) the person who says it. His attitude, influence, and future usefulness to God are hampered.

In our home the opposite is more likely to be said. In fact, we have a little family joke about it. People in the church keep coming to my wife and asking her questions about doctrine, dress, habits, and the Bible. Knowing that things sometimes work out better if the pastor answers such questions, she answers with a twinkle in her eye, "Don't ask me, I'm just the dumb preacher's wife."

Now I know her and she can say what she seems to mean a lot more clearly than that. What she's supposed to say is, "I'm the dumb wife of the preacher." (Or maybe she *is* saying what she means!)

Pastors who let things become more important than people often handicap their ministry. Handicaps like gossips, ill-informed naggers, and such are things we have to learn to live with. But pastors—and laymen—often get their eyes on material things and go astray. The pastor must always be careful that he doesn't end up at sixty-five without finances or a home of his own. He often has to do minor battle for a raise in pay. His car sometimes isn't as up-to-date as it might be. But when he lets his ministry suffer because he is concerned for these things, he cheats himself, the church, and God.

The Almighty Parent

"He'd be a good preacher, but. . . . " is a common mealtime conversation-starter. The pastor who weathers this kind of evaluation and still loves people will make it. The layman who can grow above such underhanded gossip is on the way to real maturity.

One fact that both pastor and layman need to face is that the Creator is also the Parent. He's the divine, almighty, eternal Parent of us all. And he sent his son to die for us. That's how much he thinks of people.

God made us and he provided the supreme sacrifice to admit us to heaven. People are important. People are what Christ died for.

He died for all kinds. Outside the little town of Hillsboro, Indiana, is a sign. It ought to be outside every town and city, for it "tells it like it is." As you enter the town, you are warned, "Hillsboro: the Home of 600 Happy People and a Few Old Soreheads."

That's the church. That's your neighborhood and mine. That's your job and your club and your ball team. That's life. It's filled with a lot of nice people (like you and me!) and a few old soreheads.

But Christ died for them. Don't let "things" grab your love when so many wonderful people deserve it. Don't let the soreheads of this world make you forget that human beings, created by God, are ever so much more important than the material world of things around us. People who are afraid of people hide in things. Don't let the soreheads make you hide.

Get tired by loving people. God loved them enough to give his son for them. You can at least wear out loving them.

Like the want ad in a local paper: "Girl Scout leader's hat for sale; leader worn out, hat like new."

THINK THIS IS JUNK?

Another facet of the value of people is that they can't be replaced. Things can. One antique shop has a sign in the window that says, "Think this is junk? Come in and price it."

People are of ultimate value because each is different and none can be exactly replaced.

My granddad taught Indians in the Oklahoma Territory before it became the state. His tales were hair-raising stories of terror to my young ears when I was a boy.

One story was funny. The teen-age boys all lived together on the reservation school property. Many came from distant villages where "mom" and "dad" were uneducated people who still lived in a primitive manner. These youngsters wanted the white man's education, but their culture was still pagan.

They didn't like a lot of the white man's rules—in this case the rules of Phillip Thomas Harman—and they let it be known by their actions.

Especially they didn't like the idea of "lights-out." A native Indian boy was used to being free to go and do and run when he wanted to. But granddad Harman said, "After lights-out, all boys stay in the dorm."

The boys devised dozens of slick tricks for slipping out. Granddad even started sleeping with his cot placed exactly across the one door, but time and again he'd wake up in the middle of the night and find half the boys had slipped out anyway.

The boys knew the penalty for getting caught could be expulsion from the school, but they loved to roam at night (like so many of their spiritual-heirs among modern teens).

Granddad had an inspiration. He knew by this time that the boys were only challenged by his rules. If he could outsmart them, they might respect him and abide by the rules. He wanted to teach them, no matter how he had to do it.

His plan was simple. He moved his cot away from the door and stretched a single strand of piano wire across the opening, a foot off the floor. When all was quiet and the darkness of the night covered his actions, he secured the wire in place and went to bed to wait.

Sure enough, in a few minutes he heard the "slip, slip" of bare feet on the rough wooden floor. Then a terrific "Whump!" followed by the "slip, slip" of feet heading back to bed.

At breakfast the next morning no one said a word about the night's events, but the biggest, most handsome brave in the dorm came to the breakfast table with a lump on his forehead the size of a lemon. Granddad gained the respect of the boys because he outsmarted them, and his teaching moved ahead in good style.

God has to do a lot of things to get us to serve him. But he knows our value, so he patiently works with us. Things can be replaced, but people are of eternal value.

Ever get excited about an auto race? Every time I see one, I remember how close the junkyard is to the raceway in a little southeastern Tennessee town. The best of racers end up on the junkheap sometime. But the drivers end up at the judgment bar. People are eternal. The things of earth are potential junk.

LET EACH MEMBER DO HIS THING

Strange how Paul's comparison of the church to the human body can be brought up to date in modern talk. Each member doing its special task, yet coordinated by its attachment to the head, Christ. "Let each member do his thing," Paul seems to say, "yet work together with the Man."

People are more important than things because they can add to, move ahead, improve, and enrich life itself. They can respond and react to each other and jointly make an immeasurable contribution to the life we live. Things have to be driven and governed and repaired and re-dated. Things can get out of date, but people have built-in "improvers" in each model.

A pleasant woman I know has a very select calling. She sells pickles. Actually, she's retired now, but she worked so long in pickles that she began to smell like them. But the exciting thing about the lady was that for those who knew her the odor of pickles on her was a reminder of her love and generosity and hospitality. She was hostess to hundreds of visiting preachers, educators, and guest speakers who came to work in her church. They all felt the loving care of "Miss Barbara." Her odor of pickles became a reminder of something very genuinely Christian. She "did her thing" and made the people she met love the aroma that went along with it. A meal at Miss Barbara's home was an event to be remembered, and the odor of pickles faded in importance in the presence of her love.

People can be used of God: that makes them valuable. The use God makes of persons transmits itself in strange, undefinable ways. It might have been a revelation of truth when a paper in Tennessee noted, "A good attendance was present Sunday morning. The Reverend J. A. Goodman has been sent to another church."

If we each fill our place, trust God to make our place fit in with all his other plans, and then leave things in his hands, life will work out the way he wants it. When we start checking on the other fellow, worrying about our place in the scheme of things, and second-guessing God, we find trouble.

No one's perfect in filling his place. My dad is a fine teacher and scholar and a pretty fair preacher in his way. But he has a handicap. He preaches too long.

I recall a sermon he preached that should have ended all sermons (it was long enough to do it). About forty-five minutes into the sermon—when dad was just getting warmed up—mom took out her watch and waved it at him. He ignored her for awhile, but she persisted so long that her waving took his mind off the sermon.

He paused, then launched into a very exciting story: it must have been about headhunters or something. Just at the most terrifying part, he stopped cold. Addressing the congregation in a quiet, detached sort of way, he said, "Now my wife is waving her watch at me, telling me it's time to stop. If there are any of you who want me to finish this story and keep preaching, please hold up your hands." Of course, at that vital part of the story, everyone wanted to hear the end, so they raised their hands.

In a voice filled with triumph, dad addressed mom from the pulpit and said, "See, honey, I'm not preaching too long. They all want me to keep right on." He preached another half hour and mom sat in frustrated silence.

People are alive and heading into the future. You are people. Believe in them—including yourself—and wrap your life around them. They're worth every minute of it. No matter how oddly they fill their special place!

Chapter 8

MY WIFE IS DECOMPOSED

Ever get apologetic about your home? Or feel like saying, "Help! Something's wrong in my home and I don't know what to do about it"?

Welcome to the club! Oh, I know, Christians aren't supposed to get in jams, have husband-and-wife blow-ups, have staring-and-silence periods, and the like.

But take it from any pastor you meet that such things do happen and they happen in Christian homes. To say "Christian" about a home is to say that the people there are trying to live for Christ and keep Christ central in their lives.

It doesn't mean they're always successful or not human.

Like the Christian husband who attended Sunday worship alone after a Saturday night argument with his wife. He didn't want to tell the pastor she was sick, so he thought he'd use the term *indisposed*.

Instead he blurted, "Sorry to come alone, pastor, but my wife is decomposed."

COOL IT

First step in seeing the right side of family problems is to see that some disagreements (fights, arguments, spats, rumbles, differences of opinion) are to be expected in marriage but are not to be extended or tolerated for any length of time.

First, we "cool it." Stop the fussing as soon as possible, if you want to survive. In all families arguments come when each person thinks he's right.

Cool it—maybe that's what the classified ad in an Idaho paper meant. "For sale: Cemetery plots, Cloverdale Park, near tower. Also deep freeze for large family."

The larger the family, the greater the joys, and the more opportunities for disagreements. Take this view of marriage and the ensuing family: being married is the toughest single interpersonal challenge in our lives. We are expecting two different people from two separate families with two entirely different backgrounds to leave their lives behind them and settle down in one house to live in love for the rest of their lives.

As one church bulletin announced, "The pastor will meet at 7:30 Monday to discuss marriage as a vocation and a scarement." The intended word, of course, was *sacrament*.

It's almost too much to expect. Makes you want to say "Amen" to the Pennsylvania newspaper reporter who wrote of a visiting speaker, "Obviously a man of sound judgment and intelligence, Mr. Rau is not married."

But love conquers and people *do* marry. And if Christ is the head of the house, we can expect ultimately to look back on many happy years of rich family life.

But when the ripples come, hold steady, wait, and look for a chance to repair the damage. If we don't cool it as soon as we can, we only deepen the rift. Cut off the argument and wait for things to cool down. That's the first step in healthy feuding in the home.

SHIFT GEARS

Isolate the ones having the disagreement. If it's husband and wife, get rid of the children for awhile. Get the whole situation down to the minimum of involvement. Let the Mrs. wash the dishes and the Mr. watch TV or vice versa! Cool it, and shift gears.

Start a conversation on "safe" ground. If the difficulty was over money, talk of cleaning the basement. If the trouble is over the children, talk about the fun you two had when you were dating. Start out fresh on a different subject.

Make up your minds independently that you're willing to put up with each other. Then find some common ground to help you back into harmony again.

One of the ample sources of argument in my home when I was a boy was the basement. The simple basement. But in our home—the finest home you'd ever find insofar as spiritual influence was concerned—the basement was far from a simple place. Dad made it into a chaotic tragedy. Dad's a commercial artist, and every imaginable art form, art aid, and art exhibit is stored in our basement. It is a lower form of pollution. Only dad can find his way in and out and around in it.

When he and mom had a disagreement about the basement, they'd settle it with (1) a cooling off, (2) a kiss by dad, and (3) a big show of cleaning out the basement and making it a "decent place to live in" again.

The strange thing is that the basement was a wonderland for children. The "mess" that was there never bothered them and dad had a talent for teaching moral principles through some of the art exhibits that were there.

For instance, there was "Johnny Smoker." This was a device for making a cardboard man smoke a cigarette; the smoke traveled toward his "lungs," and on the side was a fishbowl. The smoke, forced into the partially-filled fishbowl, formed a cloud over the water. The goldfish in the bowl soon had cigarette-smoke oxygen settling in the water. In a few minutes the fish would turn over and die. Dad used this device to show the dangers of smoking, long before the *Reader's Digest* and the American Cancer Society took up the cry.

But he still cleaned out the basement when mom fussed, because he knew that keeping things straight *was* a vital part of homelife, even when the "mess" could be used to teach gospel truth.

Having a disagreement? Shift gears. Talk about something else. Agree on something. Let the healing love that is a part of family life come to bear on your lives.

A TRAIN HELD BY A BOW

Marriages are fragile at their weakest link. As one description of a wedding put it, "The bride had a four foot train, attached to her waist by a small bow." It's an accurate description of the attire, but also a pretty true picture of the weight and seriousness of marriage.

One step toward repairing and redeeming the troubles of married life is to value that marriage highly and do all you can, positively, to help the marriage. It will die of neglect if you don't.

One aging grandmother with poor circulation sits up cautiously in her bed each morning before rising. Her first words are, "I'd better sit here a minute and get myself together." It helps to keep her from getting dizzy and losing her balance when she gets up.

But the same formula helps marriage itself. Take time to "get yourselves together" before deciding or changing or reacting.

No one knows what marriage is all about till he's married. One step further: no one knows the headaches and heartaches of having children till he has some. (Nor the joys and pleasures and satisfactions, either.)

Two men were riding past an elementary school one morning; the flashing red light announced, "15 MPH Zone, but the driver kept up his 30 MPH speed.

"Mind slowing down, friend?" his passenger asked.

"Why should I? There aren't any children in sight."

The passenger insisted. "Yes, I know, but we all need to get in the habit of slowing down every time we pass a school."

The driver was a little irked. "All right, but I don't understand it."

The passenger smiled. "Well, you don't have any children, but I do. In fact, I have two children in that very school. It makes a lot of difference how you drive by the school when some of your own family attend there."

And there you have it. No one knows your family the way you do. Value it. Prize it. Take care of it. When difficulties arise between members of the family, do what needs to be done with the purpose in mind of acting in the best interests of a family in which you have a personal stake. It's yours. If you don't protect, cherish, and value it, no one else will.

In a world where troubles seem to be normal, work toward peace, harmony, and a spiritual dimension that shows. One news item that pictures clearly the world's view of homelife was this:

> "Colonel and Mrs. R. J. Mason celebrated their twenty-eighth wedding anniversary with an informal gathering at their home over the weekend. The affair ended with the usual arguments."

EVER PLAY CHESS?

I'm no good at it. But chess is a great game. It helps you think ahead. Now there's no guarantee that this will have any carry-over value in marriage, but looking ahead ought to be a part of the husband-wife relationship always.

In chess there are thousands of possible combinations of moves within the first few minutes of the game. Each decision you make is unchangeable. If you touch a piece on the board, you have to move it. Once you've moved it, you can't change your mind. The key is to visualize what the board will look like if you were to make a certain move, and then guess what move your opponent will make in return. Looking ahead means everything.

Looking back in marriage helps, but looking ahead is priceless. We can save a lot of heartache if we will perfect the art of looking ahead.

A woman whose husband was known to be strong and healthy appeared at the cemetery one day dressed in black. A friend there asked in shocked disbelief, "My goodness, has your husband passed away?"

The woman answered with a sigh, "No, not *this* husband. *This* husband is so mean that I'm here mourning for my *first* husband."

Looking ahead involves loving the family, loving Christ, and picturing what will happen if you decide in certain ways. The key to this is the leadership of the Holy Spirit, for in the vast majority of life's situations, we just can't see what's ahead.

But he can. And the troubles which arise among members of the family today can be submitted to him and he can map out the right decisions that will take care of future troubles. As in all of life's activities, family difficulties can best be remedied by submission to Christ.

Chapter 9

I TURN MY EYES BACKWARD

The midweek paper from the church was a good one. Lots of interesting newsnotes and a breezy approach that caught the eye. But, alas, the pastor-editor got carried away in his column.

"As I type this, I hear birds singing, the dew is sparkling on the grass. I feel as though I am climbing a mountain. As I reach the crest, I turn my eyes backward. . . ."

That's enough. The altitude must have gotten him. His eyes swiveled in their sockets!

But like the good pastor who wrote so sincerely, all of us like to fly away sometimes. We like to soar and glide in the beauty of something-other-than-what we're-used-to.

We all get the feeling, "Boy, am I getting in a rut!"

Our habits and patterns of life have soured us on life. "Stop the world—I want to get off," expresses our feelings. Well, let's look at habits. Let's see what's good and bad about them.

SUMDAY IS COMING

Do you know what the second graders call the day when the arithmetic test is to be given? "Sumday." And on that day they sing the "Sumday Serenade."

Well, for all of us "sumday" is coming. The day of the big test. The day of accounting and challenge, and even doubting on the part of those around us. And, all too often, that day is the day our habits catch us.

Like the person who secretly uses profanity. It will pop out one day and the habit will embarrass him. The odd habit known only to close relatives will explode out in public one of these days. All of us may be victims of habits which will catch up with us sooner or later.

Many stories are told of preachers who stretch a truth, using the justification that they're trying to accomplish good. One singer paused in the middle of a song titled, "When Mother Prayed," and confessed to the audience in his most confidential tone, "Friends, my mother has prayed for me for hundreds and hundreds of years."

Another old-time evangelist got in the habit of exaggerating so often that some of his brethren in the ministry cornered him and asked him to stop. "Brethren, this thing has been on my heart, too. I want to stop. Why, I've shed barrels and barrels of tears over it." The friends gave up on that note.

76

You and I have to face the fact that we're human. Habits are a vital force in the life of humans. We need to face this and determine not to form any habits which, if revealed, will do harm to God's work. Be careful what habits you develop, the day will come when the world will see them.

The old gimmick of associating a new person's name with something about him so we can more easily recall the name in the future is a habit worth developing. One man, however, got caught up in the habit.

He was a pastor in California and as he shook hands with one parishioner, he recognized the face, but couldn't remember the name. The man was a tailor named Taylor who had made a pair of trousers for the pastor. Mr. Taylor smiled and asked, "How do they fit?" Thoughtfully, the pastor stopped to think.

After he used his recall-by-association habit, the pastor brightened and answered, "They're just fine, Mr. Pants."

Another pastor warmly assured his people from the pulpit, "I'm ready to serve you at any time. Just call me. My phone is by my bedside and you can reach me there, day or night." He surely doesn't sleep *all* the time!

Dogs That Cannot Bark

The Amplified Bible translates Isaiah 56:10, "They are all dumb dogs, they cannot bark."

What kind of dogs can't bark? Dumb dogs, yes. But

also dogs who have been so frightened by owners with sensitive ears that just when you need the dogs to bark in time of danger, they are afraid and cannot.

Habits are like that. They bind you. And just when you need desperately to do something the right way, your habits keep you on the wrong track. A mother says it: "Dear, practice good manners at home and when we're eating out, you won't be embarrassed."

Sometimes very sincere persons sense defeat in their lives after they surrender to Christ. One man, with tears in his eyes, confessed to his pastor, "Pastor, several years ago I gave my heart to Christ. Then, little by little, I took it back. One day I woke up and found I had it all. Christ had none of my heart. There was nothing left for him. Now I want to give it back and take my hands off."

Habits that catch us and strangle our spirits need this treatment. Surrender them to Christ, and hands off. Let them stay gone. Let the habit be broken. Break the tie that binds you to the habit and have done with it. It matters not whether it's a habit of speech, or action, or one of cultural compromise; give it over to God and take your hands off. Have no further communication, contact, or discussion with the habit.

The use of tobacco was a prime target for many preachers just a few years ago. But, recently, the general public and concerned health officials have taken up the cry and are confirming what the church has said for years. The habit which involves the necessity of nicotine being taken into the body is one that must be broken quickly, decisively, and permanently. There's no promise of comfort or joy in breaking it, but the mind and soul must control. You know that breaking it is right, so do it on that basis, not on your feelings, discomfort, or inconvenience.

Some people have the complaining habit. Dizzy Dean gave a sharp word to ball players who had the habit of questioning every call of the umpire. "You got just two chances to win an argument from an umpire. Slim and none." Break the complaining habit. It does no one any good.

Remember, habits *will* catch you, and if they're bad habits, they can ruin you. They'll bind you and doom you.

Pray for Rain and Mow the Yard

But the useful and redemptive fact about habits is that if they're good habits, they can save you.

When we have the habit of believing in God, we can do like the old farmer recommended to the city-dweller when he complained about a drought. "Well, son, if you believe in God like I do, just pray for rain and get out the mower. It'll start raining soon."

When we get the habit of believing in God, we act like it. We make the habit serve us, instead of strangling us. We work hand in hand with God in de-

79

veloping the right way and then get in the rut of being God's person. We start with the old Virginia Negro preacher's request, "Lord, prop me up in all my leaning places," and we move ahead. God starts us off right and we get in the rut of being his kind of person. Then in a tight spot the habit rescues us.

Clarence Hatch was a marvelous Christian leader and a tremendous example to his family. Some of his habits of right living were derived from his father, a Nebraska wheat farmer.

Clarence used to tell of the time on the farm when the wheat was ready for harvest on a Saturday. "Rain and hard wind forecast for Sunday night and Monday. We better get up early Sunday and get this wheat harvested," Clarence told his dad.

"No, son," his dad answered. "We're a Christian family and we go to church on Sundays." Their rural life meant that going to church was an all-day affair.

"But, dad, if we wait till Monday, the storm may ruin the crops. And besides, all our neighbors will be out in the fields tomorrow."

"No, son. Church is a habit with us. We'll wait and see. But on Sunday we'll be in church."

Sure enough, Sunday saw them in church and one of Nebraska's worst thunder and wind storms hit the area Sunday evening. By Monday the wheat was ruined.

With a warm smile Clarence would tell the story. He'd finish it with, "Dad lost the crop, but he saved his sons." Three of them entered the Christian ministry and two daughters married ministers. His habit may have cost him money, but it paid off richly in Christian witness.

Habit Is the Key

Perhaps the most dramatic use of this habit-serving-you principle is in the story of Ben Hogan. As most people know, Ben is one of the all-time greats of professional golf. A number of years ago Ben was in a terrible auto accident. The doctors said, "Your playing days are over." But Ben wasn't convinced.

At 135 pounds, there isn't much to Hogan. In 1948 he was on top: he won the U.S. Open. Then the accident. But, to the sheer delight and surprise of everyone, Ben came back to win the United States Open again in 1950 and '51. In 1953 he did the impossible: he won the United States Open, the Masters, and the British Open, all in one year. How did he do it?

Habit is the key. He calls it, "muscle memory." In short, Ben said to himself, "How *should* this shot feel if I were to make it perfectly?" He took each shot, step by step, and trained his twisted and drawn muscles to "feel" the shot, step by step. Then he drilled his muscles till they automatically did it the way it was supposed to be done, thus bringing each muscle back to where it was before the accident. He had made a habit of doing it right; then, in professional competition, his muscles "remembered" how to do it.

You can do it for your soul: try prayer, witnessing, remembering scriptures. Any spiritual exercise that is worthwhile, you can train your mind to do. Then God can use your habit when it suits his purpose to to do so. The habit can save your usefulness to God.

What will it be: habits that doom you or habits that save you? You choose. You can make them your master or slave.

Chapter 10

BLESS EVERY PHRASE

The teacher threw down the book. "Who in the world writes this stuff, anyhow? I can't understand it, so how am I supposed to teach it to those children?"

The scene is familiar. The teacher has waited too long to start preparing, and now the whole lesson and the lesson plan make no sense. Throwing down her teaching aid in disgust, the teacher wonders who could write such terrible stuff.

You've seen it happen. Maybe you've felt it. Or said it. Or perhaps written a letter to "someone in charge" complaining about the material.

Let's look at this written-word section of Christian knowledge to see what we can discover.

First, remember that everyone makes mistakes. The public speaker can laugh aloud at his, with his audience, and perhaps turn a disaster into an interesting highlight to his talk. But the printed word is there for everyone to see, read, reread, and—hopefully— enjoy many times over. The written goof dies a thousand deaths before it's forgotten.

For example, a news item revealed this vital bit of modern technology: "About one-third of all passengers flying between London and Paris travel by air."

Or, from a midweek church paper: "Scouting program for boys, girls, and cubs." (Watch those animals!)

Or, the pastor's column with a bit of poetic license: "As I type this, the sun is coming up full." (Sometimes it's empty?)

Or, from a Sunday worship folder: "Will all mothers planning to have babies in the service next Sunday, please inform the pastor in advance."

Or, pity the plight of the worship service chairman who read from the worship folder: "Do men light a candle and put it under a bustle?"

Everybody makes mistakes, but you and I, with good cause, respond a lot more openly to those we read, for the written word can be proofread and checked and revised.

Yet, the complaint of the Sunday school teacher was not one of error but of poor material. Let's look at the written word and try to get it in the right perspective.

As a pastor listened to a woman pray, he smiled. Thinking of the unfinished manuscript in his typewriter, he murmured, "Amen." The deeply sincere woman prayed, "And God, please bless every phrase of our work." He knew she meant "phase," but the unwritten phrases of his Sunday school lesson manuscript haunted the pastor. He did need prayer. He knew the written word needed saturation in prayer. Every phrase of your church's teaching material needs prayer.

MEETING OF THE BORED

Someone has described a church committee as a "meeting of the bored." That may be true of some committees. But always remember when you revolt against the "poor" material in the church's printed resources that it most assuredly was done by a coordinated, hard-working group. And while you may feel you do not receive much inspiration or help from it, others will feel differently.

It's almost impossible for dedicated, knowledgeable men and women of God to create Christian materials without a depth of blessings being laced through each page. Somebody will be helped by that "poor" material, whether you are or not. My personal experience with most complaints is that the persons who complain —not the materials—lack something.

Not every lesson outline, every article, every printed pamphlet from the church publishing house will be just what you need, but it will fit what many people need. Don't be too disappointed if it fails to inspire you. (Or, as one author-pastor announced to his people at the close of a service, "There is a wonderful book on sale in the lobby. Pick up one as you pass out.")

Somebody will be blessed. A pastor wrote a brief note to a small child who'd been sick. As an after-thought, the minister pasted a small picture of Sall-man's "Head of Christ" on one corner of the envelope. The tot grabbed the letter from the mailman and went running to his mother. "Mother, mother, look! I got a letter from Jesus!"

Writers of Christian literature in our day are among the most dedicated, the most concerned, the most sen-sitive to the needs of their readers of any group of writers in any field of journalism. They care. They pray. They seek diligently to be led of the Spirit in creating just what you need.

So, the next time you feel like throwing away ma-terials, remember that someone prayed over that material more than you have. Be kind to the writers. Don't imitate the news item that observed, "The bride-elect was showered with pieces of her favorite china."

The writers are trying to help you in your dedica-tion. In reading some of the fine stories for children that are in our Sunday school materials, I notice how engrossed in them I become. Surely the children love them. Surely the writers know—as the great fisher-men of all time know—that "More fish are caught by the tale than any other way."

THE KING JAMES VIRGIN

A few years ago we in the church endured a long, hot, and often senseless disagreement over a new version of the Bible. One of the main points of the trouble was the translation of the word in Isaiah 7:14 which the *King James* renders as "virgin." The *Revised Standard Version* says "young woman."

It was especially interesting to hear a highly inflamed preacher burst out with the promise, "It is not God's will that we have the new Bible. He will always favor the *King James* virgin!"

The next observation we need to make about Christian literature is that it aims for solid, basic, long-range building of Christian character. It's not a fancy, flash-in-the-pan attempt to win converts in one hearing. It's not built to turn minds by a few minutes of teaching. There's little of bombast or exciting novelty in the church's message. We're building for the ages. We're training for a lifetime. We're handling the most sacred part of the human being—his soul.

If the writing you see in the church isn't as appealing as some comic books, remember, it's not supposed to be!

Everything must be done to make our materials readable, interesting, and appealing. But the serious, holy, life-and-death matters which are involved in the gospel can't be transmitted or received in a brilliant flash. It takes time. There's great merit in the long-run training and molding effort of the church. Respect your materials for this serious, responsible approach.

Often the message is subtle. Often our lives as leaders, teachers, pastors, adult laymen are the indispensable ingredient in the material that holds sway in the class. The writer gives the leader the chance to back up the printed material with his example and testimony.

Paul was a roommate of mine in college. I thought he was a good friend. We got along well, until. . . . Until he met an auburn-haired beauty from West Virginia. Then his heart was wrapped around her and her alone. I'd wake up in the middle of the night to see the light on and Paul staring at Mary's photo. "I love that girl," he'd sigh.

Naturally they got married and our bachelor apartment living was ended. I still thought we'd gotten along well, till Christmas. Paul gave me a book as a gift. My illusions were dashed. The book was titled, *On Being Fit to Live With*. Sometimes the written message is subtle. And sometimes not.

THE CHRISTAIN

There's a requirement involved in using Christian materials in the church. You have to add "you" to them. As with the writers who allow the teacher, the leader, to "star" in the classroom, so in all of Christian effort, the message without the messenger is bare.

After many years away from my home church in Baltimore, I went back. After church I took a sentimental tour of the building: to the back pew I sat in as a teen-ager; to the boiler room where my dad tanned me for cutting up in class; to the junior department where my favorite teacher guided me. It was there I saw it. The activity for the day must have included wall plaques, for there they were, all in a row. I read them over. Then I laughed. One was supposed to say, "Lord, I Want to Be a Christian in My Heart." Instead, the pupil had misspelled Christian. It read, "Lord, I Want to Be a Christain in My Heart." I laughed. Then I stopped.

After all, that's what it takes, doesn't it? Having a "Christ-stain" in the heart. If we aren't touched, if we aren't cut to the heart by the seriousness of our jobs, then it makes Jesus' tremendous sacrifice rather foolish, doesn't it? His dedication should call forth a like dedication on our part.

The Christian leader is fair game for every problem known to man. We never know when something serious is going to be dumped in our laps. We're always on "standby" duty.

Ann Landers' column in one paper made this even worse for her. It said, at the close of the advice letters, "Ann will be glad to help you with your parents. Send them to her in care of this newspaper."

You, at your spiritual best, are the best preparation

for teaching, speaking, leading, and participating. Let the printed materials—with all their goofs, poor attempts at helping, and offbeat subjects—guide you. But you need to be the best disciple you can be when you take that material and use it.

Voluntarily add yourself to the framework of the church leadership post you have. You can't transmit the lesson material without becoming involved. You can't blame poor material for your poor example. You can't hide behind a lesson that's difficult or a subject that's sensitive or an approach that's unfamiliar. If you are the Christian adult you're supposed to be, God and you can handle even the worst piece of Christian literature ever printed.

Chapter 11

ONE OF OUR CARNAL DOCTRINES

Many ministers are excited about preaching on the subject of the church. And as human, prone-to-goof people, ministers often get their feet in their mouths. As one pulpit-thumping Kentucky preacher blurted out, "Why, unity has *always* been one of our carnal doctrines." He immediately realized he should have used the word "cardinal" but it was too late then.

Ever get the feeling that everyone at church is a hypocrite? "They say they have unity, but they seem carnal" might be the accusation we level at times.

We feel sometimes a kinship with the truth expressed by the sign in a store: "We Buy Old Furniture and Books. We Sell Rare Antiques." It may appear that churchgoers are hiding something, pretending to be something they're not.

How can we cope with this feeling? What can we say or do? Let's hunt for some "messages" that might help.

PSYCHEDELIC SAINTS

Church people are wild, really wild. They're all different. They're hard to figure out. They're peculiar in a hundred different ways. They're what some teens might call "psychedelic saints."

And because you and I are part of the variety of persons who love the church, we must face the fact that to others we, too, may seem wild.

We'll just have to put up with each other, that's all. Put up with the rough ones. Like the hard-to-get-along-with board member who was warned by a kindly older lady, "You better be careful or you'll get an ulcer."

He replied, "I don't get ulcers. I give them."

We'll need to adjust. Though our hearts feel the "message" of the little boy who asked his teacher at Christmas while they were arranging the stable scene, "Where do I put the three wise guys?" though we feel that way, we have to stay calm. Put up with each other. Though sometimes we share the sentiments of a Kiwanis bulletin: "We had Herb Dennis listed as absent last week. He was present and we're sorry."

Some people at church remind us of the woman who complained to the marriage counselor that her husband was so rude and nasty he ruined life for her. Even early in the morning, she felt disturbed and unhappy. The counselor asked, "Tell me, do you wake up grumpy?"

She fired back with, "No, I let him sleep as long as he wants."

The church is composed of people placed there by God. Now just because they're there doesn't mean God has finished his work on them. All of us know unfinished saints. Poorly altered people who need a lot of work done on them.

One city official in a report to the City Council was quoted as saying, "Unless we add more revenue to the budget, several school teachers are going to leave their pests."

The church is a family. And families have skeletons, black sheep, and other persons with problems. One ad for a bug-killer declared: "Effective in killing flies, aunts, and other pests."

The first thing to remember about hypocrites, troublemakers, and the like is to put up with them. They put up with you, don't they?

Daisies on the Sloop

After you've set your jaw, determined to endure other persons, then look inside yourself. Start making sure that those little "carnal" people who want to see what a real Christian is like can look to you as an example.

You show them how. Or, as one headline put it, "Egg-Laying Contest Won By Local Man." Give them something to see that tells them how it's done.

Get yourself in the best spiritual shape you can. Be as fussy with yourself as you might be if you were fixing up someone else's life. Be more precise than the message in a church midweek paper which began, "I sit here thinking of the countryside. Daisies brighten the grassy sloop." How nice: bright daisies out at sea in a sailing sloop, instead of on their familiar slope.

Adjust to the situation and adapt yourself to the needs of those around you. Make the most of opportunities. As one English church did: for over one hundred years the church had awarded prayer books to young teens as encouragement to them to practice their faith. Leaders sighed as they planned their awards for this past year, and decided to award alarm clocks instead of prayer books. Alarm clocks seemed more needed for the teens.

Adjust, and live the Christian life before those you think are playing at their faith. When I think of one who put shoes on her faith, I think of Donna. She is a beautiful girl who ultimately became a finalist in the Miss Tennessee pageant. But Donna is also a strong Christian, and losing the contest was just one of those events of which life seems full.

Donna had strong convictions against the use of alcoholic beverages. Once, on a goodwill tour of South America, she was brought face-to-face with a touchy, difficult decision. The mayor of the town she was touring presented her to a group of thousands of people and proposed a toast in wine to her. Then he offered her the drink. She stalled as long as she could, then quietly explained her convictions to the mayor. By God's help, things went all right, and Donna's simple witness was spread far and wide in the wine-drinking country.

Then, as Donna was preparing for a career as an airline stewardess, she faced another similar decision. She really wanted to work in the air terminal, but had to take the stewardess training. As part of it, she was asked to learn to mix and serve drinks to passengers. She balked. She asked to be excused from this part of the schooling. When she was informed she was required to do it, she refused.

"You will take it or clear out of our dorm this afternoon!" she was told. Donna was shocked at the harsh reaction. But, trusting in God and sure her decision was right, she packed her belongings, left the dorm, and walked slowly down a Chicago street. She had no friends and no money.

On an impulse, from God, she's sure, she called a young man she'd met in church the Sunday before. He met her for lunch and, after hearing her story, simply said, "The office where I work needs a clerk. And there's an empty apartment in our building." Six hours after Donna's ultimatum from the airline school, she had a job, a place to live, and a real friend. God took care of Donna as she trusted him with her life:

past, present, and future. By the way, she married
the friend and they have a happy home today.

A Whale of a Belly

The third key is as simple as it is old: keep your
eyes on Jesus, not on men. Ignore this, and you can
get into a lot of trouble. Or, as one pastor observed
in loud tones in the midst of a sermon on Jonah, "You
can be sure that Jonah was in a whale of a belly!"
Another "Jonah" fact to remember: "When down
in the mouth, remember Jonah: he came out all right."

Be careful. Several years ago a wealthy British
duke was telling a friend, "The other night I dreamed
I was addressing the House of Lords. I woke up, and
I was!"

Only Christ can be the example *you* need. Use him
as such. To view other people is to be disillusioned.
One man in Michigan sued his wife for divorce stating
for his grounds the fact that after four weeks of marriage, he discovered his glasses had been out of focus
since before his wedding.

People let you down, literally and otherwise. The
congregation chuckled when a "goof" in their midweek
paper stated, "A special musical part of the service
last Sunday included soloist, Mrs. Marie Tilson, who
sank two numbers."

Look at Christ. Study his life in the New Testament.
Make a personal friend of him. To know him is to
begin being like him.

The renowned warrior, Tamerlane, is said to have been trapped one day in an abandoned shack. He feared for his life and his warriors felt helpless without their leader. As he crouched low to escape detection, he saw a tiny ant trying to carry a grain of wheat up the wooden wall. His interest was kindled as he sat watching. The ant, by Tamerlane's count, dropped the grain sixty-nine times on his way up. Each time he would go back down the wall and pick it up again. Finally, on the seventieth try, the ant placed the grain on the shelf he'd been heading toward.

The warrior took heart, escaped, and led his troops to victory. To see Christ, keep working at our spiritual needs, and be the example we should be to others ought to consume our energies, attention, and time. We'll be a lot less bothered by hypocrites in the church if we'll follow these steps.

In spite of this, things will nag at us. Some things we'll have to endure. We can hear the sigh in the voice of the child psychologist who advised a mother, "You'll have to handle him with care, and remember, you're dealing with a sensitive, high-strung little stinker."

Christ is our leader. Perhaps the most heartening idea to hold fast in our minds is phrased in Proverbs. The *Living Psalms and Proverbs* paraphrases Proverbs 30:24, 27 this way: "There are four things that are small but unusually wise: [one of which is] The locusts: though they have no leader, they stay together in swarms."

How much more fortunate are we than the locusts. By instinct they stay together. Through Christ, the church must stick together in love. Love those hypocrites and trust Christ to change them. You've got enough to handle with yourself!

Chapter 12

WE REPROACH THY THRONE

All of us make mistakes. But the layman who prayed aloud in the morning service, "We humbly reproach thy throne," said more than he knew.

Ever feel that way? That your prayers weren't going any higher than the ceiling? That no one was listening? That you might just as well repeat a nursery rhyme because no one was hearing? The praying layman with the error in his words might have meant such things. Our prayers might as well be a reproach to God, for all the good they do.

But in our hearts we know this is the wrong attitude. What can we do? Prayer is the key to effective living, but how do we use that key?

So many books have been written on this and so many ideas have been fluttered about in the spiritual atmosphere that it's a temptation to repeat the admonition, "All that's needed in understanding prayer is to get people to practice it." But there's more.

Spoonerisms

First, let's look at some Spoonerisms. This term is applied to "an accidental transposition of sounds, usually the initial sounds, of two or more words." Examples are easier to show than the phrasing is to define. A Reverend William A. Spooner of Oxford, England, is credited with so many of these that they took his name.

In reference to prayer, look at these (and picture yourself saying them):

"Will you all bow your word for a head of prayer?"

"Let's stand to our heads and bow our feet."

"Bow your eyes and close your heads."

Marvin Hartman is given credit for this one: "Please, Lord, undernourish and gird these children." That prayer was prayed at a service of dedication for children of Christian parents.

You see the idea. And you've done it, haven't you? You're lucky if these examples are the worst you've done. Some Spoonerisms are rather embarrassing and some are better left unrepeated.

But these present about prayer the first thing that needs to be said.

Be Natural

Don't be self-conscious about praying. Be natural. Pray in public in a more general way than you pray in private. And don't forever whip yourself if you dislike praying in public and don't want to do so. There's no rule written down in heaven anywhere that all Christians must master the skill of praying aloud before a listening audience. Even if we follow the suggestion of one pastor: "If you don't like what you hear when I pray, then don't listen. I wasn't speaking to you, anyhow. I was speaking to God."

If you're called on to pray when you haven't had advance notice, keep it short, simple, and sincere. Avoid the "King James Plague." (That's the feeling that in speaking to God you have to use Old-style English with "thees" and "thous" throughout.) The best policy is simply to tell the leader in advance that you will work for the church in any way God wants you to, but that you don't feel called on to lead in public prayer. He'll understand. He also has areas where he isn't so comfortable or proficient.

Spoonerisms are a natural part of public speaking. Every speaker has said them. You will, too. If not in prayer, then in some public comment during a discussion. Or over the phone to an important person. They're part of life. If you face this, then you may feel more at ease in praying in public.

BE SINCERE

The second thing to be said about praying is this:

Our feelings in prayer are secondary to our sincerity. The feeling that "my prayers aren't getting anywhere," needs to be answered with, "And *where* are they supposed to get?" If God is omnipresent, it means he's in the room with you. Getting prayers to go "as high as the ceiling" is all the farther they need to go. In fact, as many mature Christians know, some of the most effective prayers are not even heard by anyone's ear. They're the quiet prayers we say in the heart. (My wife calls it "praying to yourself," and she won't change the phrase even when I remind her that we pray to God, not ourselves.)

God is with you as you pray. The sincerity of the heart is overwhelmingly more vital than the feelings or the emotions. I'm never sure that tears in prayer are any sure sign of effective prayer. Just saying words out loud that speak of our troubles is a great relief. In psychology it's called catharsis. We air our troubles and feel better for it. It may or may not be prayer. It may or may not include the ear of God. Feelings in prayer are dangerous measuring rods.

Our earnest desires to (1) contact God, (2) seek an answer to our need, and (3) bring ourselves in line with God's will, are what matter. Sincerity, not emotional satisfaction, is a key in prayer.

Like the small boy sitting on the curb in a big city repeating the alphabet over and over, letter by letter. A teen-ager came by and listened to him. "What in the world are you doing?" asked the teen-ager.

"I'm praying."

"But you're not. You're just repeating the alphabet."

The boy looked up and answered, "I know it. But I'm just in the first grade. I don't know how to pray. But I know the alphabet and I trust God. I'm saying the letters and letting him put them together like they ought to be."

BE COMFORTABLE

The third significant idea about prayer is this:

There are things we want to express to God that are unspeakable. Some yearnings can't take form as words. We can't say them aloud, because they aren't made up of words. They're vague fears, half-hopes, groping desires, heartfelt yearnings. We "feel" toward God and trust him to understand what we mean. Let's not be defensive about this. Let's practice the belief in God's omniscience. If he knows all, let's treat him as if he does. We can't fool God, and we know it.

But also, we can feel perfectly comfortable in saying to him, "You understand how I feel about this matter," and *know* that he does! No counselor would settle for such a statement. No prayer-partner could ever know enough to sense what we mean. But God does. There are some unsayable things in prayer that we ought to keep in mind when we kneel.

This came to mind when a pastor asked, just before the morning prayer during a worship service, "And are there any unknown requests this morning?" Everyone knew he meant "unspoken" but he conveyed more than he realized. There are "unknown" requests and feelings and dreams that we have, and it is right to take these to God in prayer.

BE PERSISTENT

The final observation about prayer is this:

If your way of praying brings results, stick with it. The incomparable Frances Gardner Hunter tells of learning to pray in a bathtub. More power to her! If the tub is where you feel closer to God, pray there. If the closet or bedside or out behind the garage is the place you feel you reach him, go there.

Carroll Dale, all-pro flanker back of the Green Bay Packers, wrote to a trusted Christian friend, "Pray for us Sunday. It's a tough game." The letter, unfortunately, didn't arrive till the Monday after the tough game. The Packers already had lost when the Christian friend got the letter.

The answer came back to Dale: "If you want results in prayer, get your requests in on time. I prayed for your next game and you won." Dale answered back with a simple list of all the remaining games, with the note, "We need help in all of them."

If it works, do it.

One wonderful Christian woman in Kentucky heard the doctor diagnose "cancer." It frightened her. As the time drew near for surgery, Elsie appealed to her Sunday school class for prayer.

The Sunday morning before surgery, one lady in Elsie's class stood and said, "I feel that God would have us all stand and surround Elsie and pray for her." Class members felt somewhat ill at ease standing and encircling the sick woman, but they did it. After they prayed, each assured Elsie of continued concern and prayers.

To the surprise of all, surgery was not necessary. Elsie was healed. And you can believe that this Sunday school class will forever stand up and surround its members whenever serious prayer needs are felt.

That's the way they do it. It works for them. We all know that the secret is not in the standing, but in the faith and trust in God. But if you have found a way to strengthen your faith and it is consistent with all you know of God's will, then hold on to it.

Don Ritchey, national leader of men and an executive with Marathon Oil Company, tells of a memorable prayer experience in his life.

Don had been asked to teach a class of juniors in his home church. What seemed like a simple job became tough as he tried to relate to the children and reach them with the gospel. Frankly, he was rather discouraged.

One Sunday morning Don woke up with symptoms of a serious illness. He called his replacement and stayed in bed, thinking what a flop he'd been for his junior class.

Then, in midafternoon, a knock sounded at his front door. Mrs. Ritchey opened the door and admitted a boy who said simply, "I am in Mr. Ritchey's class at church and I've come to pray for him." The surprised lady ushered the lad into her husband's room.

"I've come to pray for you," he announced. He knelt, prayed, arose, shook hands with Don and left. Nothing complicated. Nothing profound. He felt concerned, came, prayed, and left.

Don soon recovered his health. But more, he saw that his work for God with that class was not only worthwhile, but that somehow he had conveyed the heart of the gospel. He learned the formula: see the need, take action, do what's needed, and leave the results to God.

After all, that's what prayer's all about anyhow, isn't it?

Get the message? I hope so.